THE LEGEND OF ZELDA™
Series

D1296472

Produced by
Alfred Music Publishing Co., Inc.
P.O. Box 10003
Van Nuys, CA 91410-0003
alfred.com

Printed in USA.

ISBN-10: 0-7390-8281-7
ISBN-13: 978-0-7390-8281-2

Guitar arrangements by Satoshi Aikawa, under supervision by Nintendo.
TM and © 1986–2009 Nintendo

THE LEGEND OF ZELDA™
Series
for Guitar

CONTENTS

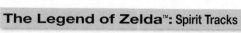

THE LEGEND OF ZELDA™:
TITLE THEME

Composed by KOJI KONDO

Original Key = B♭m

THE LEGEND OF ZELDA™:
MAIN THEME

Composed by KOJI KONDO

Original Key = B♭m

♩=110

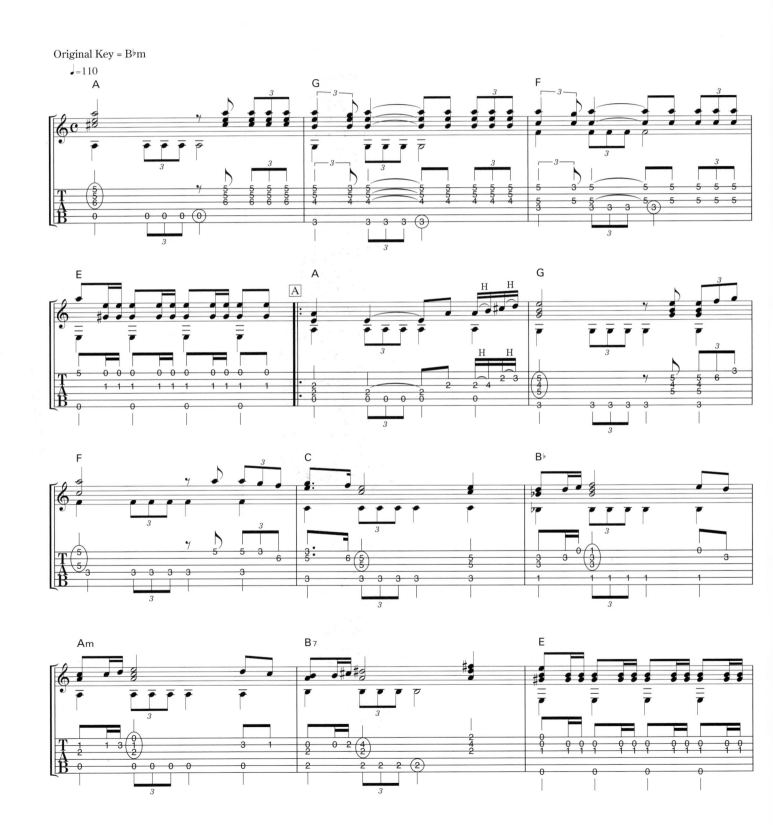

THE LEGEND OF ZELDA™:
TRI-FORCE FANFARE

Composed by TORU MINEGISHI

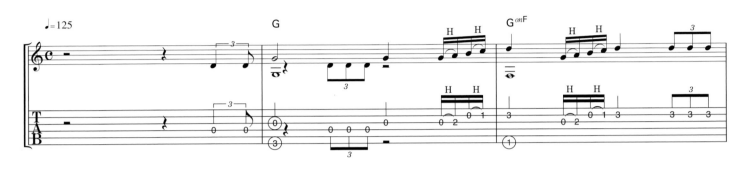

THE LEGEND OF ZELDA™:
CORRECT SOLUTION

Composed by TORU MINEGISHI

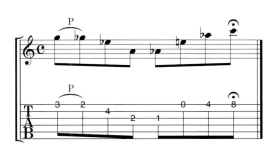

THE LEGEND OF ZELDA™:
WHISTLE OF WARP

Composed by TORU MINEGISHI

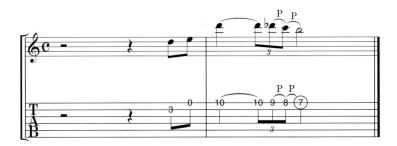

ZELDA II™:
The Adventure of Link™
TITLE THEME

Composed by AKITO NAKATSUKA

Original Key = F

♩=105

ZELDA II™: The Adventure of Link™
PALACE MUSIC

Composed by AKITO NAKATSUKA

Original Key = Gm

♩=135

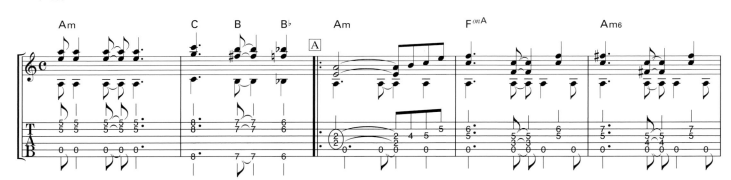

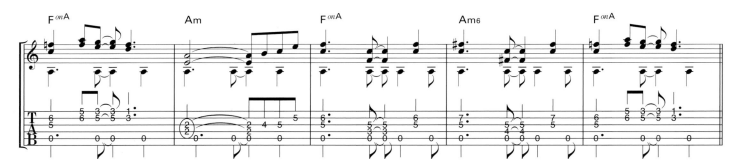

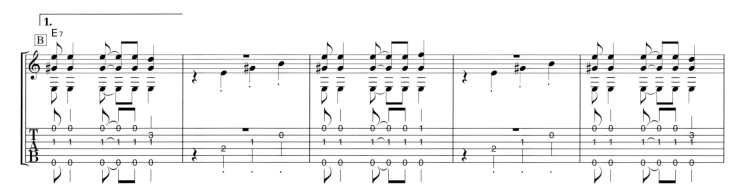

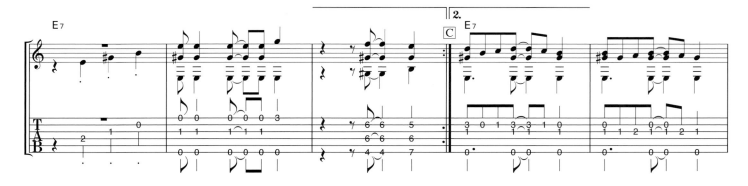

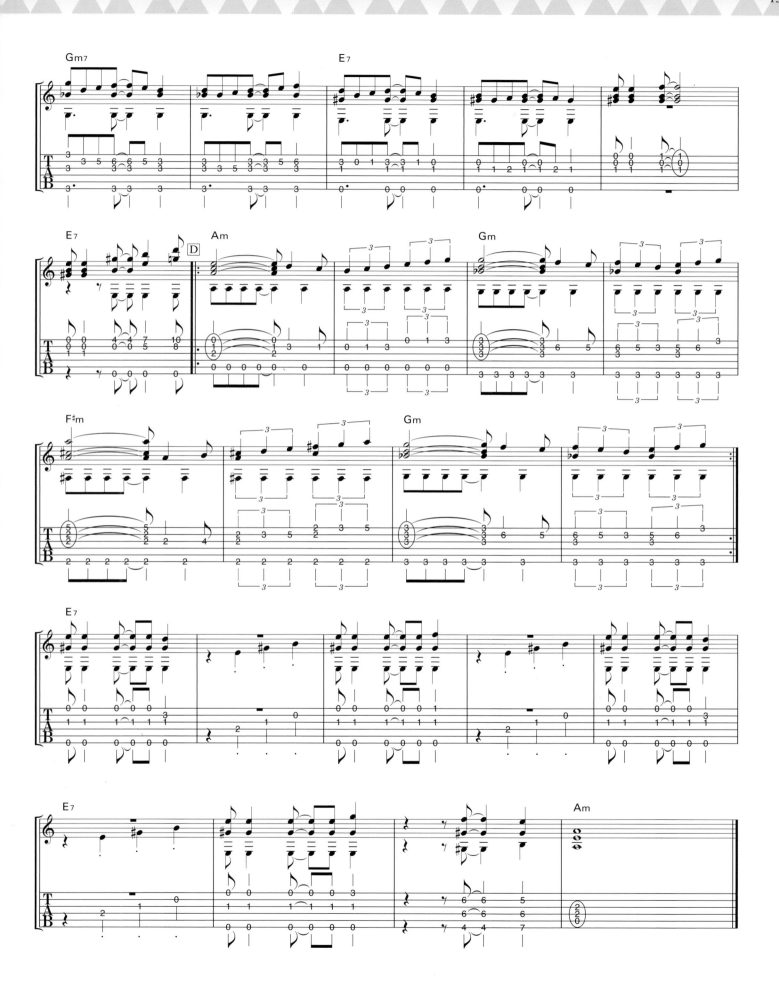

THE LEGEND OF ZELDA™:
A Link to the Past™
TITLE SCREEN

Composed by KOJI KONDO

Original Key = A♭

Rubato

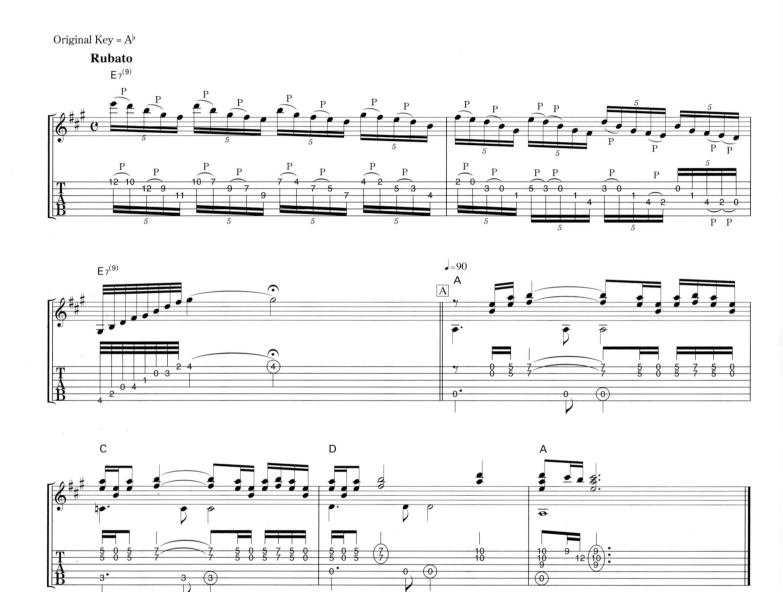

THE LEGEND OF ZELDA™:
A Link to the Past™
HYRULE CASTLE MUSIC

Composed by KOJI KONDO

Original Key = Gm

♩=110

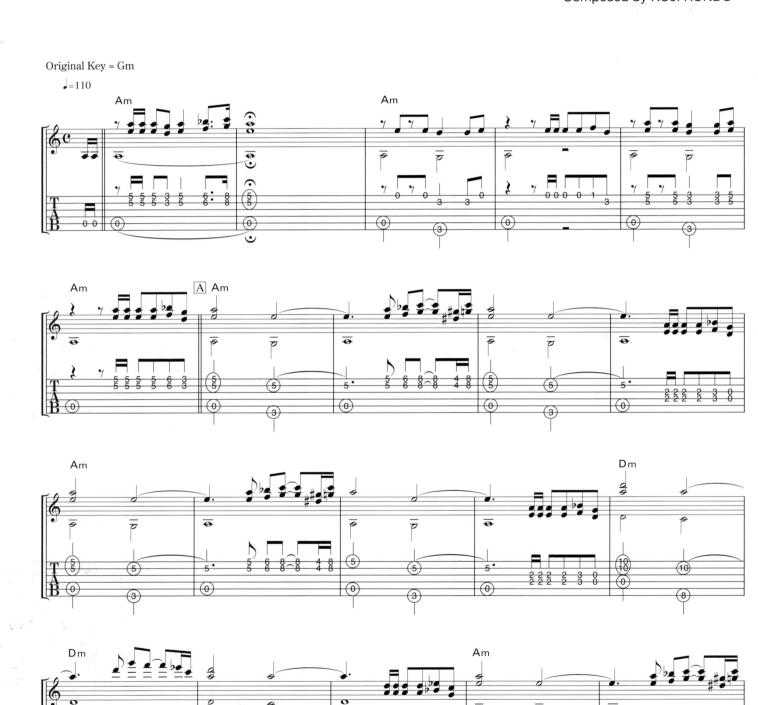

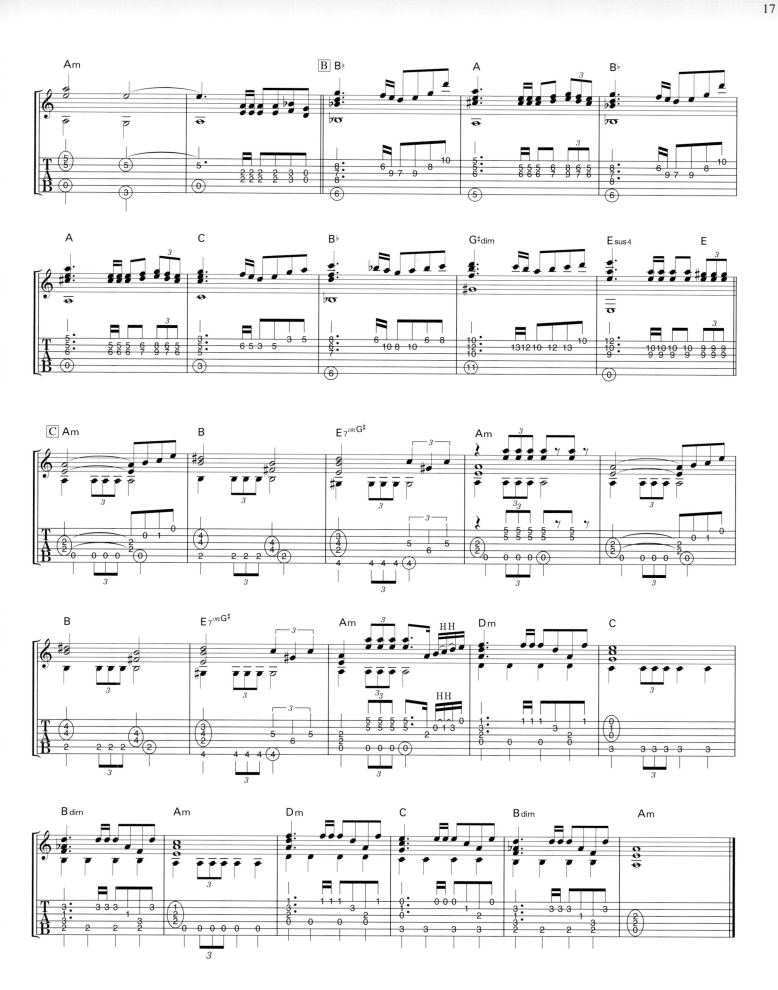

THE LEGEND OF ZELDA™:
A Link to the Past™
MAIN THEME

Composed by KOJI KONDO

Original Key = B♭m

♩=110

THE LEGEND OF ZELDA™:
A Link to the Past™

THE DARK WORLD

Composed by KOJI KONDO

Original Key = Cm

♩=110

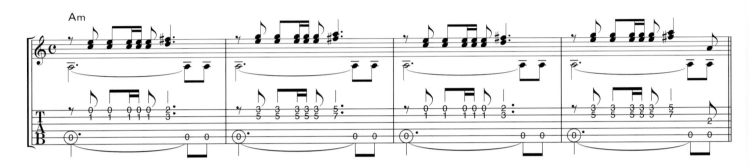

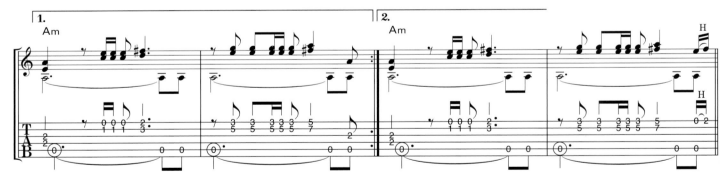

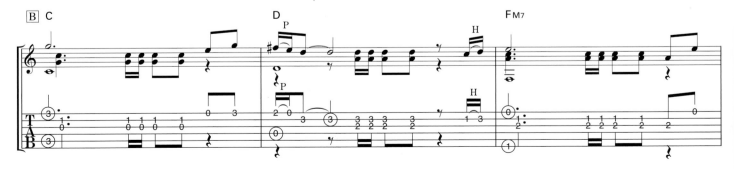

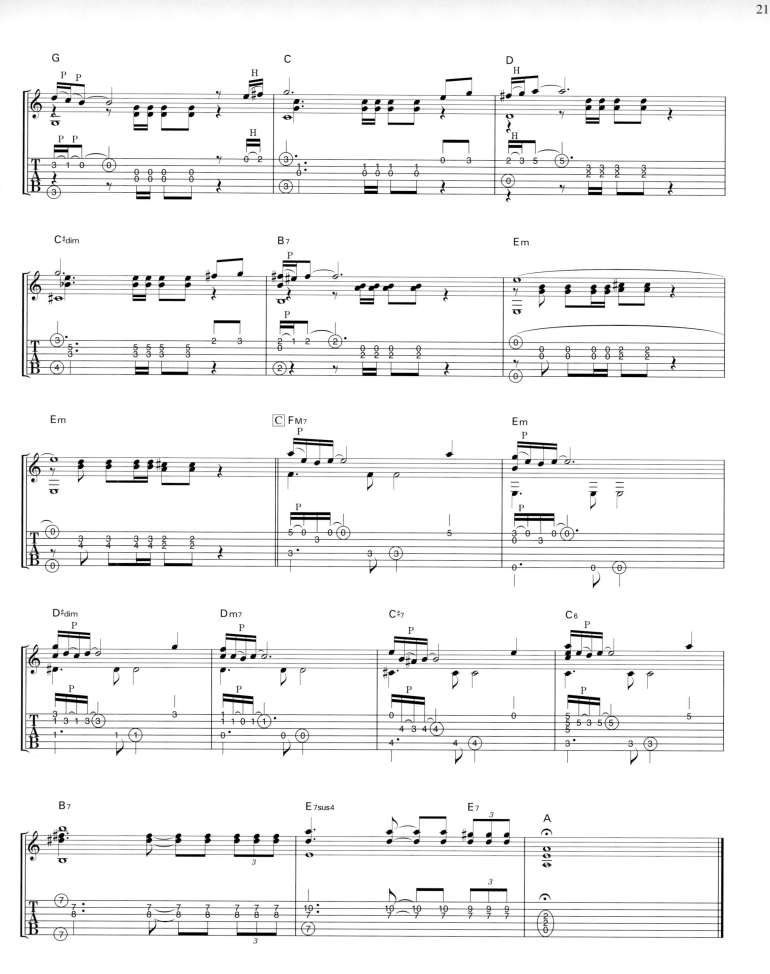

THE LEGEND OF ZELDA™:
Link's Awakening™
MAIN THEME

Composed by KOJI KONDO and KOZUE ISHIKAWA

23

THE LEGEND OF ZELDA™:
Ocarina of Time™
TITLE THEME

Composed by KOJI KONDO

Original Key = C

♩=80

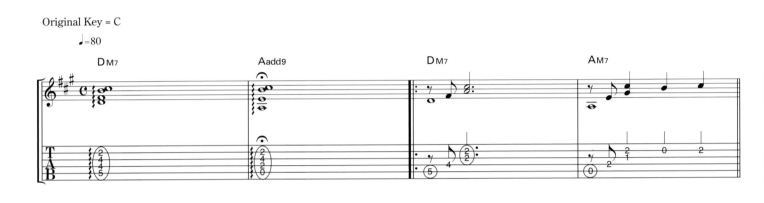

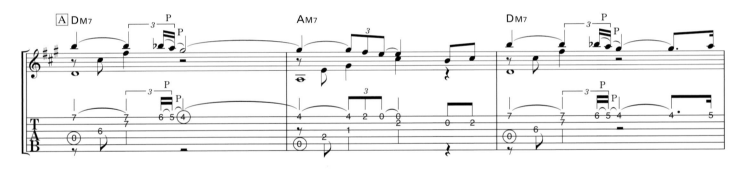

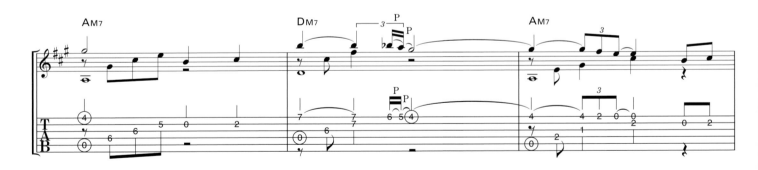

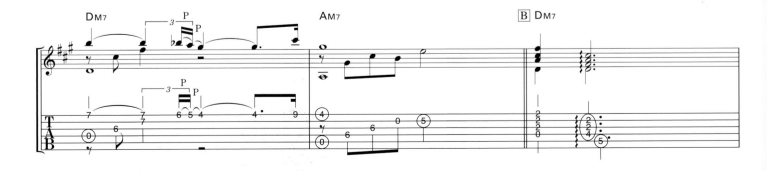

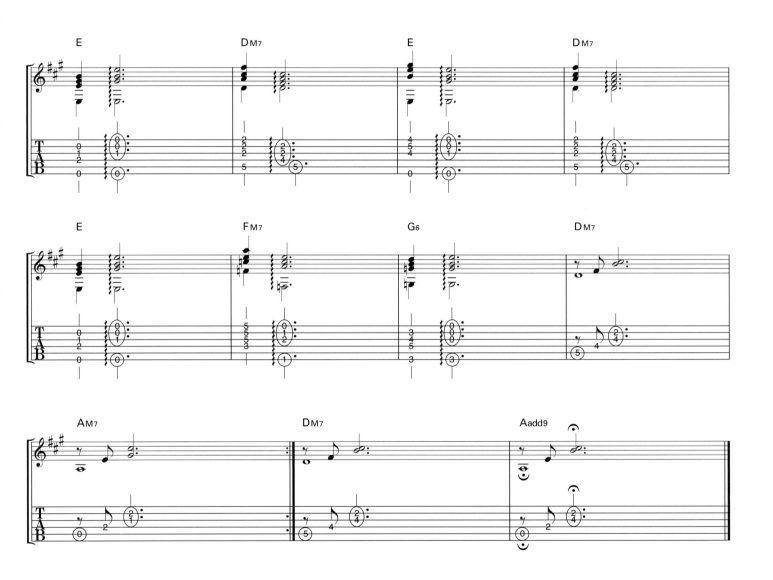

THE LEGEND OF ZELDA™:
Ocarina of Time™
LOST WOODS (SARIA'S SONG)

Composed by KOJI KONDO

Original Key = C

THE LEGEND OF ZELDA™:
Ocarina of Time™
HYRULE FIELD

Composed by KOJI KONDO

THE LEGEND OF ZELDA™:
Ocarina of Time™
SONG OF STORMS

Composed by KOJI KONDO

THE LEGEND OF ZELDA™:
Ocarina of Time™
GERUDO VALLEY

Composed by KOJI KONDO

Original Key = F#m

♩=110

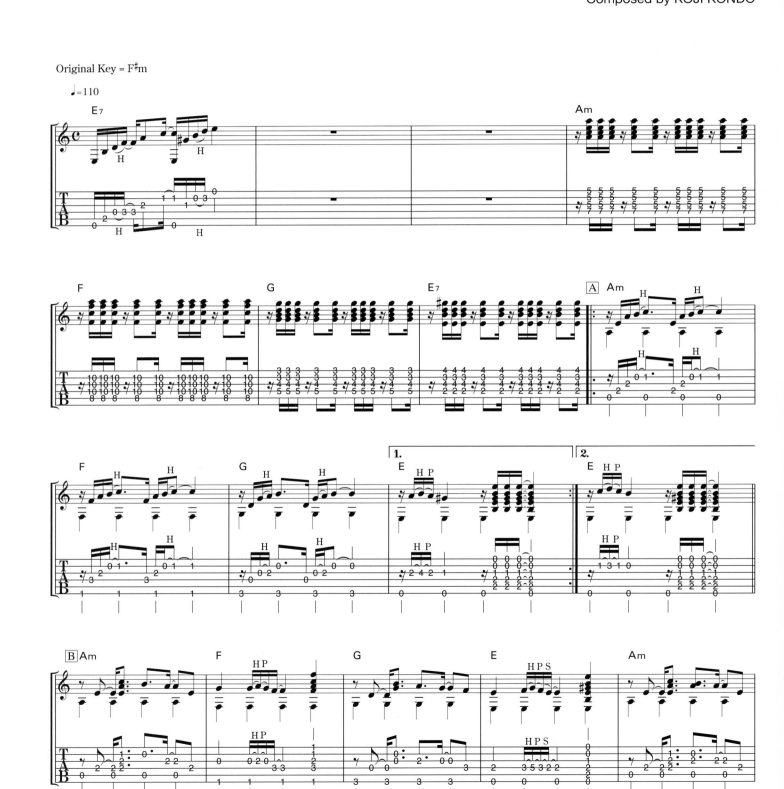

THE LEGEND OF ZELDA™:
Ocarina of Time™
PRINCESS ZELDA'S THEME

Composed by KOJI KONDO

THE LEGEND OF ZELDA™:
Majora's Mask™
PRELUDE OF MAJORA'S MASK

Composed by KOJI KONDO

D.S. al Fine

THE LEGEND OF ZELDA™:
Majora's Mask™
TERMINA FIELD

Composed by KOJI KONDO

Original Key = Gm

In Tempo ♩ = 105

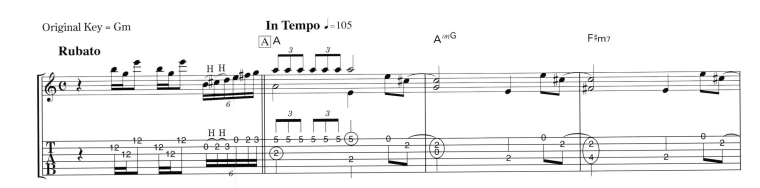

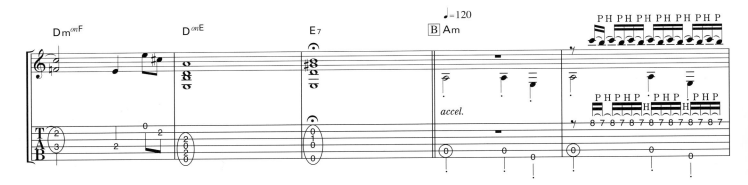

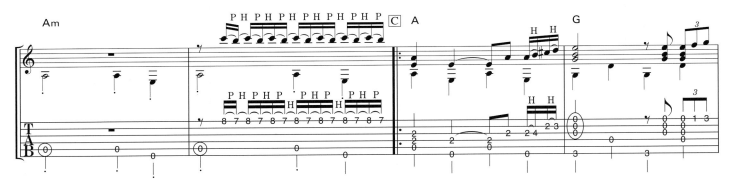

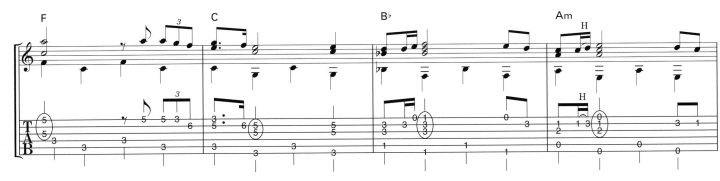

THE LEGEND OF ZELDA™:
The Wind Waker™
MAIN THEME

Composed by KENTA NAGATA

Original Key = D♭

♩=110

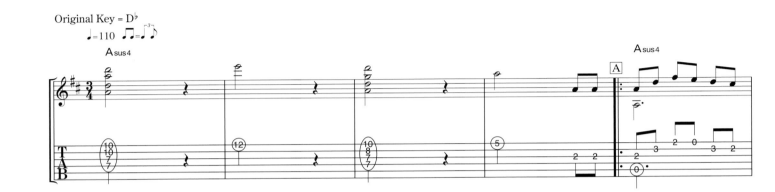

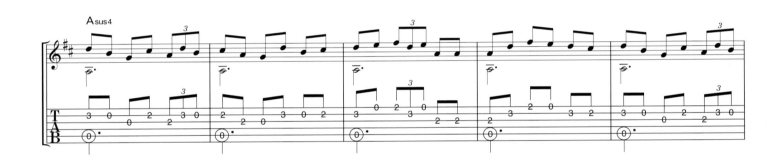

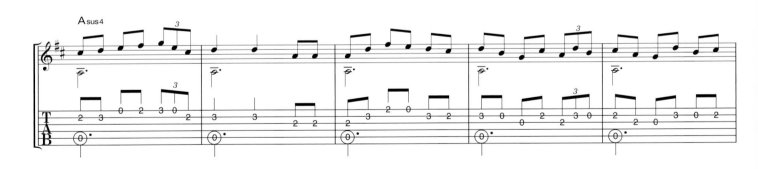

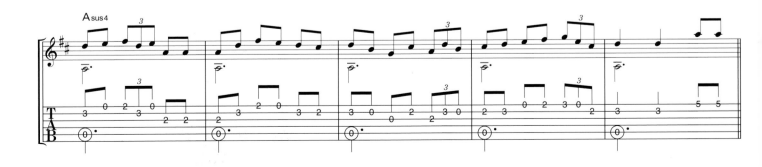

THE LEGEND OF ZELDA™:
The Wind Waker™

DRAGON ROOST ISLAND

Composed by KENTA NAGATA

Original Key = Gm

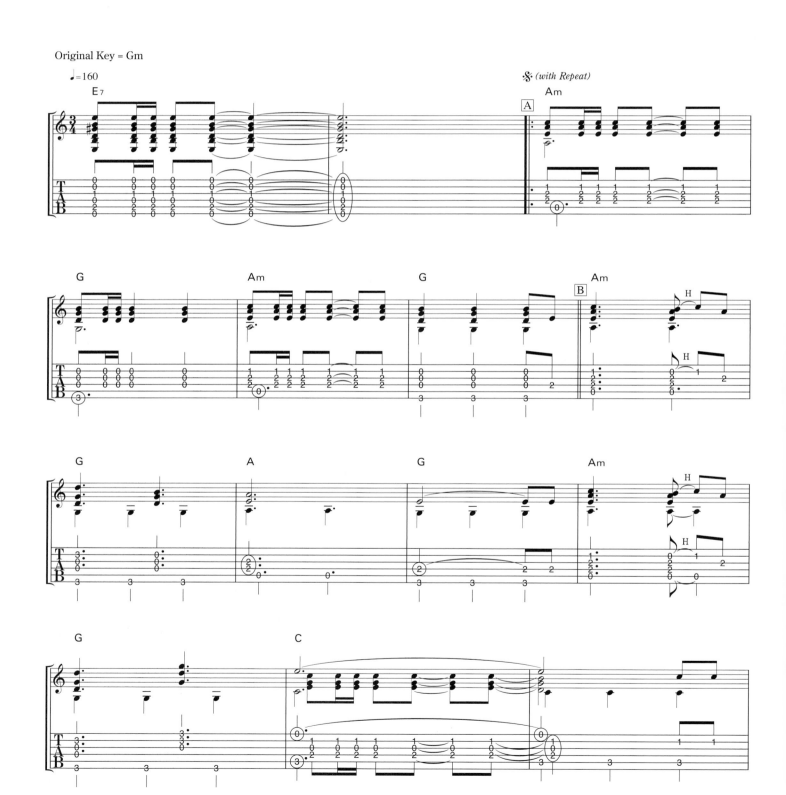

THE LEGEND OF ZELDA™:
The Wind Waker™
OCEAN THEME

Composed by KENTA NAGATA

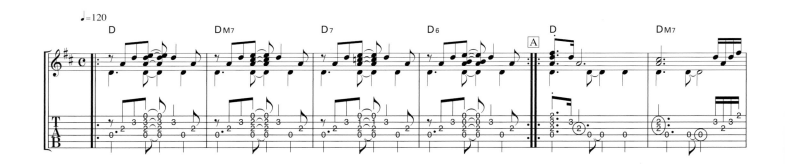

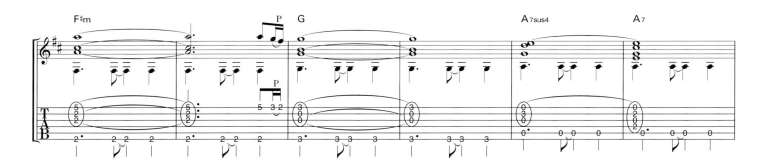

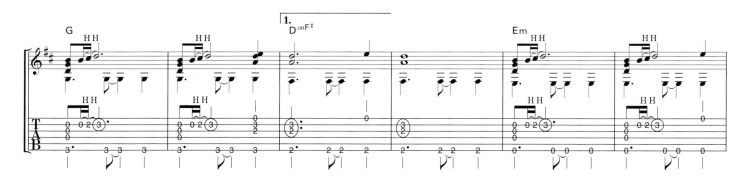

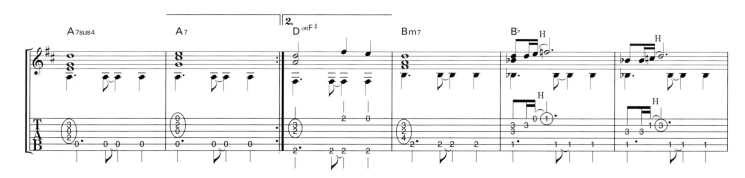

THE LEGEND OF ZELDA™:
The Wind Waker™
MOLGERA

Composed by HAJIME WAKAI

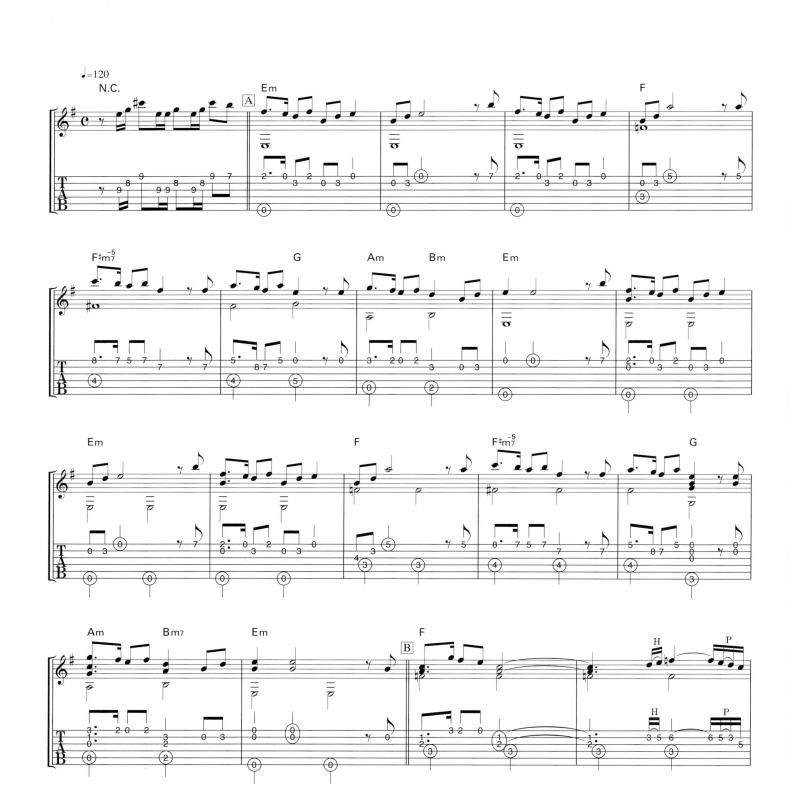

THE LEGEND OF ZELDA™:
Four Swords Adventures
FIELD THEME

Composed by ASUKA OHTA

Original Key = G

♩ = 120

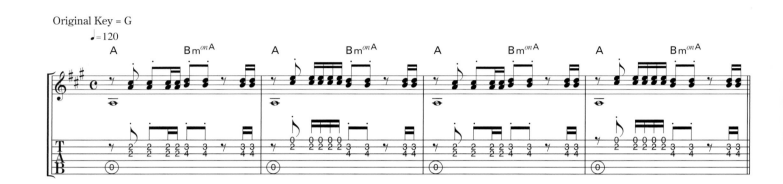

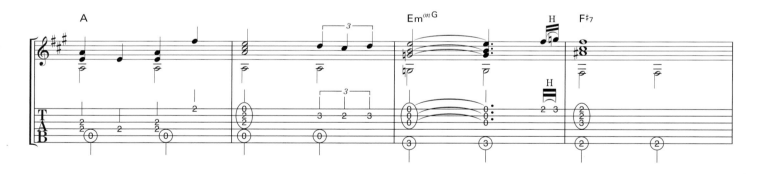

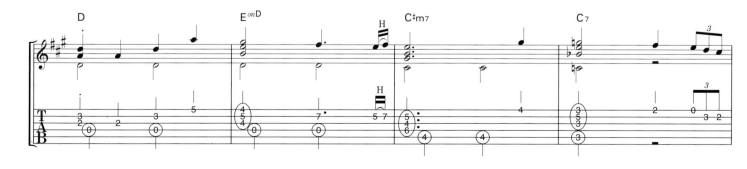

THE LEGEND OF ZELDA™:
Four Swords Adventures

VILLAGE OF THE BLUE
MAIDEN RESTORED

Composed by KOJI KONDO and ASUKA OHTA

Original Key = B♭m

♩=130

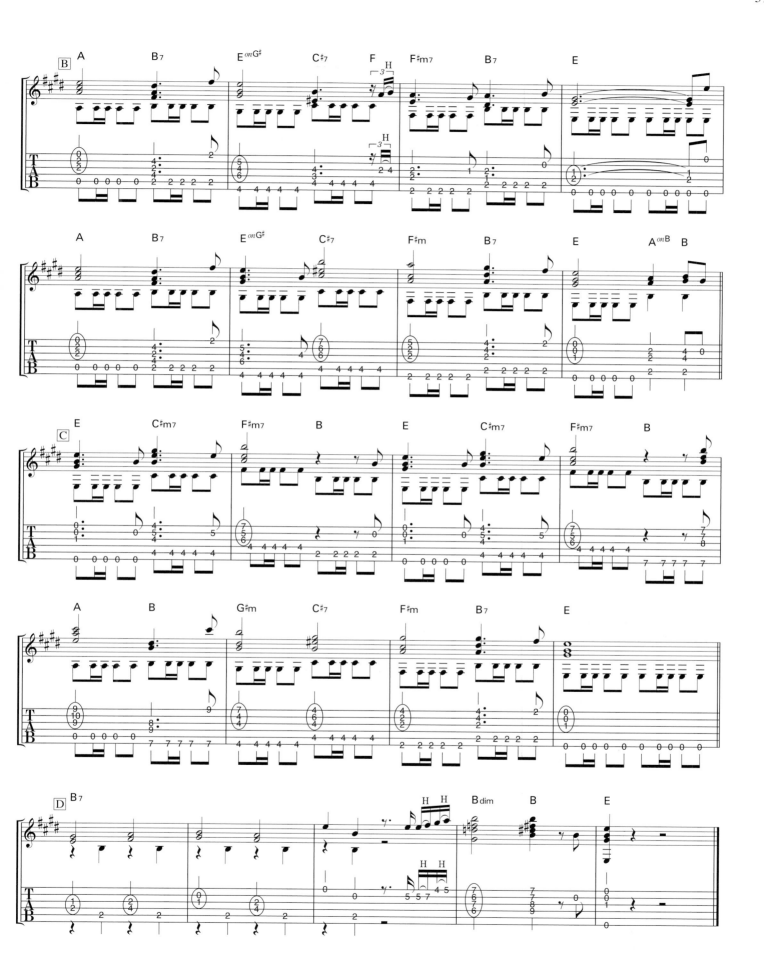

THE LEGEND OF ZELDA™:
Twilight Princess
HYRULE FIELD MAIN THEME

Composed by TORU MINEGISHI

THE LEGEND OF ZELDA:
Twilight Princess

HIDDEN VILLAGE

Composed by TORU MINEGISHI

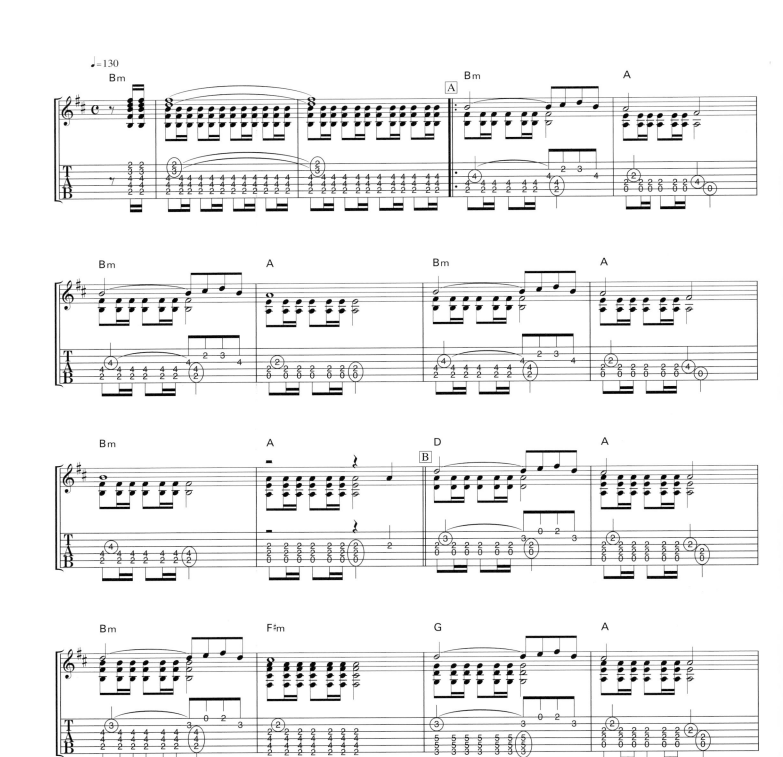

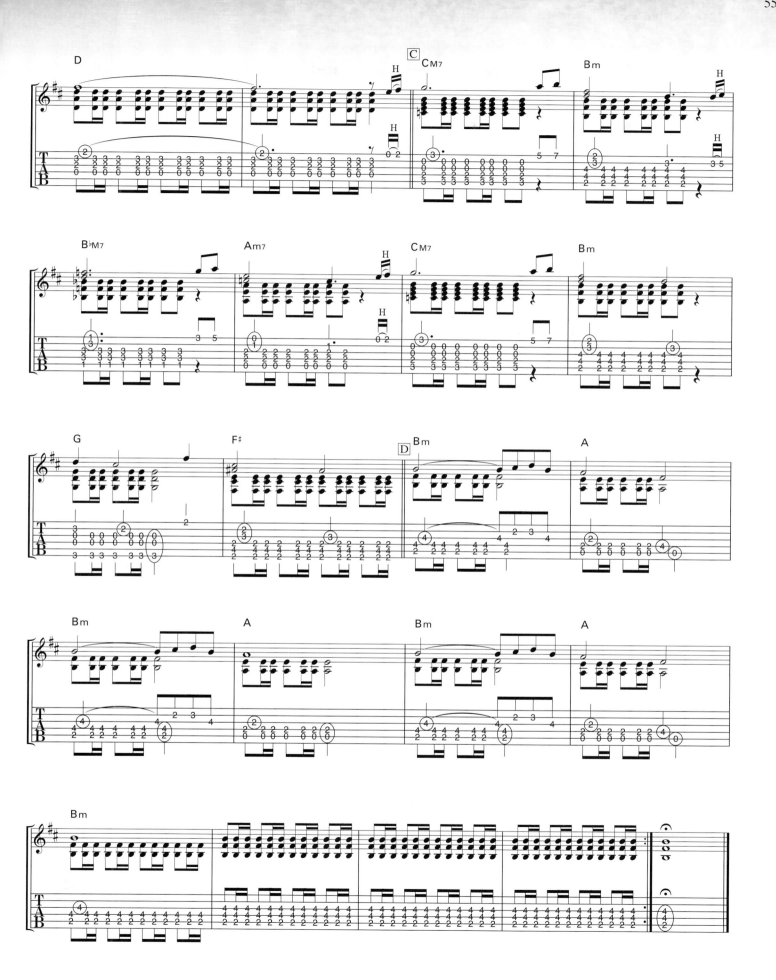

THE LEGEND OF ZELDA™:
Twilight Princess
MIDNA'S LAMENT

Composed by TORU MINEGISHI

Original Key = Dm

♩=100

THE LEGEND OF ZELDA™:
Phantom Hourglass
CIELA'S PARTING WORDS

Composed by KOJI KONDO and TORU MINEGISHI

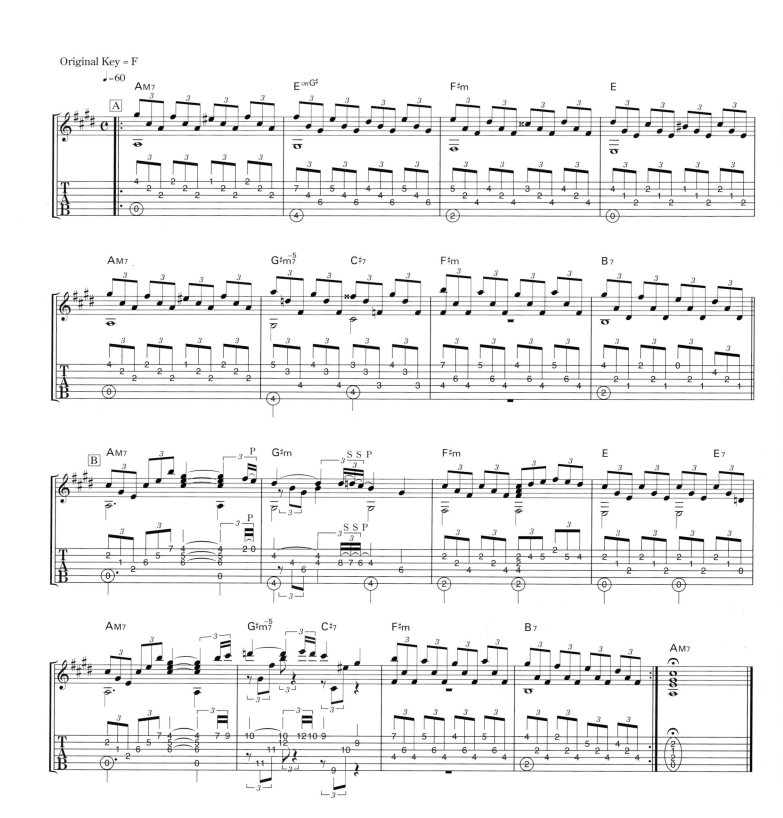

THE LEGEND OF ZELDA™:
Spirit Tracks
FIELD THEME

Composed by MANAKA TOMINAGA

THE LEGEND OF ZELDA™:
Spirit Tracks
TITLE THEME

Composed by TORU MINEGISHI

THE LEGEND OF ZELDA™:
Spirit Tracks
TRAIN TRAVEL (MAIN THEME)

Composed by TORU MINEGISHI